W9-BYC-971

One Vol. 4

Created by Lee Vin

Translation - Surah Kim Schultz
English Adaptation - Marion Brown
Copy Editors - Peter Ahlstrom and Hope Donovan
Retouch and Lettering - Christina R. Siri
Production Artist - John Lo
Cover Design - Harlan Harris

Editor - Julie Taylor
Digital Imaging Manager - Chris Buford
Pre-Press Manager - Antonio DePietro
Production Managers - Jennifer Miller and Mutsumi Miyazaki
Art Director - Matt Alford
Managing Editor - Jill Freshney
VP of Production - Ron Klamert
President and C.O.O. - John Parker
Publisher and C.E.O. - Stuart Levy

A  Manga

TOKYOPOP Inc.
5900 Wilshire Blvd. Suite 2000
Los Angeles, CA 90036

E-mail: info@TOKYOPOP.com
Come visit us online at www.TOKYOPOP.com

One is © 1999 Lee Vin, DAIWON C.I. INC. All rights reserved. First published in Korea in 1999 by DAIWON C.I. INC. English translation rights in North America, UK, NZ, and Australia arranged by DAIWON C.I. INC. English text copyright © 2004 TOKYOPOP Inc.

All rights reserved. No portion of this book may be reproduced or transmitted in any form or by any means without written permission from the copyright holders. This manga is a work of fiction. Any resemblance to actual events or locales or persons, living or dead, is entirely coincidental.

ISBN: 1-59182-755-8

First TOKYOPOP printing: October 2004

10 9 8 7 6 5 4 3 2 1

Printed in the USA

Volume 4
by Lee Vin

HAMBURG // LONDON // LOS ANGELES // TOKYO

•ONE VOLUME 4•

Behind the Music...

Now that Jenny has gotten Eumpa's foot into the door of the music world, it's on to auditions! After one small step for the boy and one giant step for boy band-kind, Eumpa becomes the lead vocalist of the Next One team. But since musical talent isn't in the spotlight of this new group, Eumpa must learn to set the dance floor ablaze... or be dropped because of his lack of bop.

This is Korea's top TV personality, Jihae Han...
It took them awhile to digest the fact that Jihae Han came here to sign the contract as Eumpa's guardian.

Also, they realized that when Eumpa makes his public debut...
...this could cause a huge scandal.
JIHAE-- YOU'RE JIHAE HAN, RIGHT? HOW DID YOU BECOME EUMPA'S GUARDIAN?
I'VE BEEN TAKING CARE OF EUMPA WITH HIS PARENTS' CONSENT.
HERE'S THE CONTRACT.
LOOK--YOU WANT THE TRUTH?!

EUMPA IS SECRETLY MY ILLEGITIMATE SON!
HA! I'M JUST MESSING WITH YOU! I WOULD HAVE GIVEN BIRTH AT 15...

It was cold...

IT COULD BE TRUE, THOUGH.

ARE YOU READY TO ORDER?

IT'S POSSIBLE.

She might have lied about her age!

The president watched too many soap operas, and the director read too many graphic novels.

DON'T WORRY ABOUT THE POTENTIAL SCANDAL. I'M TAKING CARE OF HIM UNTIL HE MAKES HIS DEBUT, BECAUSE HE HAS NO OTHER PLACE TO GO.

host or hosted event above
event is Kab's own
event formed.

we make two copies of the
contract

1999, June 12

Company Name: Issue Productions
The President: Youngji Choi
Address: Chungdam-dong,
Kangnam-gu, Seoul
Name: (Guardian) Jihae Han
Registered Residence Number:
Address: Yeonhee-dong,
Seodaemun-gu, Seoul

WHERE SHOULD I SIGN?

SINCE I'M EUMPA'S GUARDIAN, I WON'T BE HAPPY IF YOU SCREW HIM OVER.
THANK YOU VERY MUCH.
AREN'T YOU GOING TO ORDER?
MENU
SLURP!
Eumpa Won. Concluded exclusive contract with Issue Productions.

TAKE GOOD CARE OF EUMPA, MR. YUNJIN.

LOOK, I NEED TO TALK TO YOU.

LISTEN...

WHAT'S GOING ON? WHY ARE YOU HIS GUARDIAN?

WHY ARE YOU HIS MANAGER?

I'M GOING CRAZY.

WHY DOES THIS HAVE TO BE SO COMPLICATED?!

TELL ME THE TRUTH. WHAT'S YOUR RELATIONSHIP WITH EUMPA?

HE'S MINE.

FIRST, THE PRESIDENT PUT OFF THE DEBUT OF TEAM ONE, AND NOW JIHAE IS EUMPA'S GUARDIAN...

WHAT THE HELL'S GOING ON HERE?

I HEARD THE PRESIDENT ISN'T MOVING FORWARD.
IS HE SCARED?

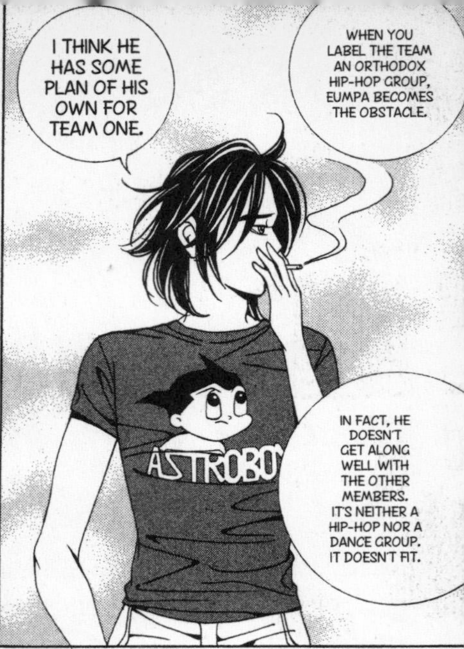
I THINK HE HAS SOME PLAN OF HIS OWN FOR TEAM ONE.
WHEN YOU LABEL THE TEAM AN ORTHODOX HIP-HOP GROUP, EUMPA BECOMES THE OBSTACLE.
IN FACT, HE DOESN'T GET ALONG WELL WITH THE OTHER MEMBERS. IT'S NEITHER A HIP-HOP NOR A DANCE GROUP. IT DOESN'T FIT.

YUNJIN, YOU SHOULD DO SOMETHING UNEXPECTED.
GET THE PRESIDENT OFF HIS ASS!

USE ME.
WHAT?
THEY'RE SO FREAKED ABOUT THIS SCANDAL WITH ME AND EUMPA. I THINK YOU SHOULD BE THE ONE TO LEAK IT.
THE BEAUTIFUL WOULD-BE SINGER LIVING WITH JIHAE HAN.
HIS FATHER, JAEKYOUNG WON... HIS MOTHER, YUMI HAN... THE GENIUS WHOSE MUSIC WAS STOLEN BY WOOJAE HA...
ASTROBO

HAVEN'T YOU FIGURED OUT WHY WOOJAE MADE SUCH A PRODUCTION OVER THIS?
WHY DID HE...?
COMING OUT!!
THE TWISTED GENIUS WHO WAS BORED TO DEATH FINALLY FOUND HIS TOY!
NOW, HE WANTS THAT TOY ALL TO HIMSELF.
RANDEUR
DIDN'T YOU KNOW THE REASON THAT WOOJAE JOINED SD, THE RIVAL OF ISSUE?

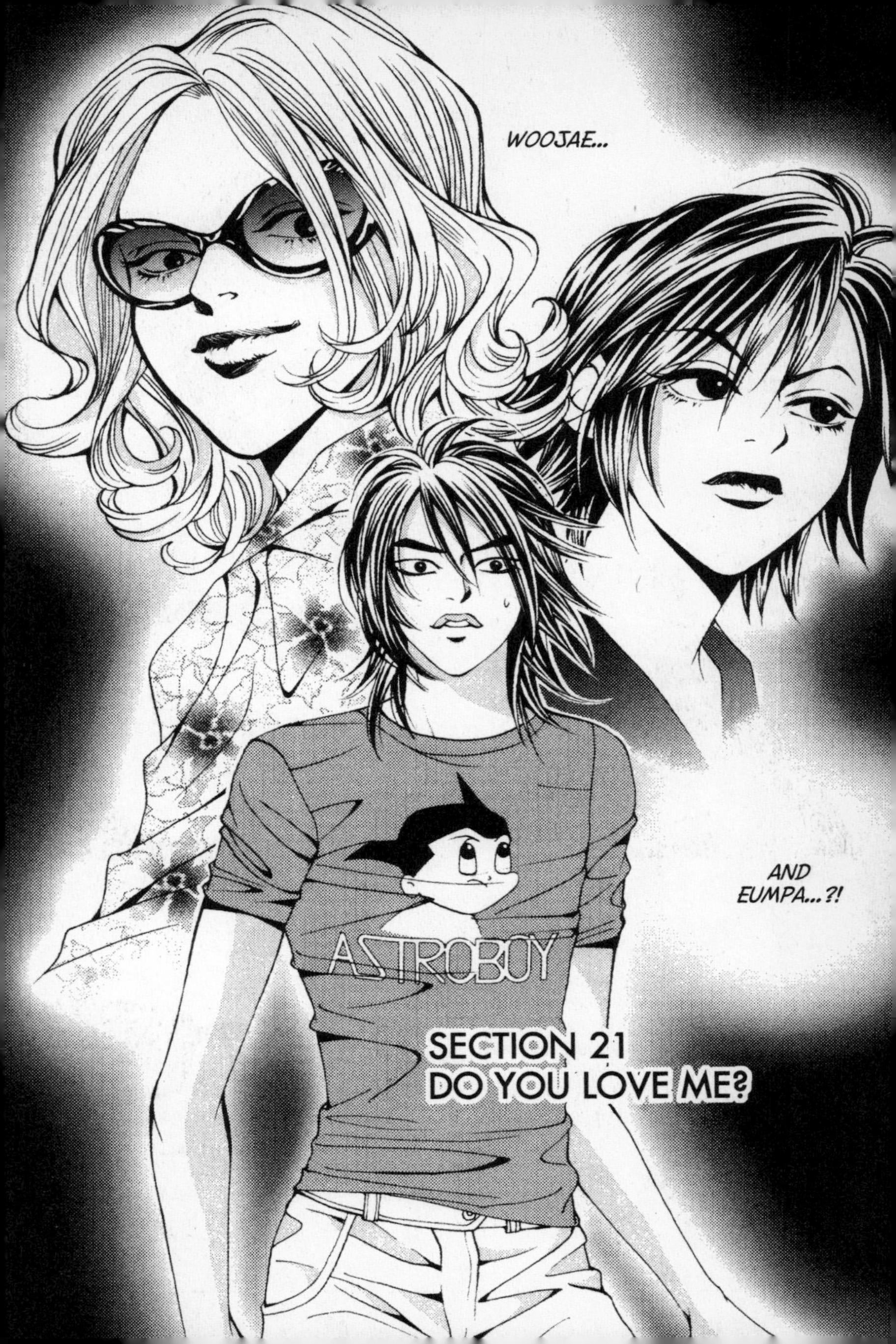
WOOJAE...
AND EUMPA...?!
ASTROBOY
SECTION 21
DO YOU LOVE ME?

WHY...

MAYBE WOOJAE LOVES EUMPA.
WHAT'S UP WITH THIS GIRL...?
HOW ABOUT YOU?
I TOLD YOU THAT HE'S MY SON.
WHY DO YOU WANT TO DAMAGE YOURSELF TO HELP EUMPA GET NEWS COVERAGE?
I WANT TO MAKE HIM A STAR. NO MATTER WHAT!

JIHAE!
ALL THE TRUTH WILL COME OUT AT THE PRESS CONFERENCE...
MY SCHEDULE IS TIGHT. I HAVE TO GO.
ASTRO
I FOUND A REMARKABLE BOY IN MY MUSIC CLASS TODAY. HE'S EITHER A GENIUS OR AN IDIOT.
I SAVED A PLACE FOR YOU, BUT YOU NEVER SHOWED.
WE'LL MEET AGAIN EVEN IF WE'RE NOT FRIENDS...
WOOJAE...?

SD MUSIC

NO. I HATE IT!

WHAT DO YOU WANT? STOP WHINING.

WHAT I HATE MOST IN THE WORLD IS TO SEE A GIRL WHINING.

I TOLD YOU I HATED BEING A MEMBER OF A GIRL BAND.

I WON'T DO IT AGAIN!

HAVING A PONYTAIL ON BOTH SIDES OF MY HEAD, DANCING AND SINGING WITH AN ULTRA-HIGH VOICE ...
SINGING CHEESY SONGS LIKE "I WANT TO BE YOUR GIRL"... ♬ BLAH BLAH BLAH. I ABSOLUTELY REFUSE.
NICE CLAUP
ANGIE.
SO WHAT IS IT THAT YOU WANT TO DO?
I WANT TO SING REAL MUSIC.
I WANT TO SELL MY VOICE AND MUSIC, NOT MY FACE AND BODY.

I WANT TO BE AUDITIONED FOR YOUR SUPER GROUP.
ARE YOU CONFIDENT?
YEAH.

I MET A GIRL LIKE YOU...
...IN MY HIGH SCHOOL MUSIC CLASS.
JENNY YOU.
SHE'S ORIGINAL. SHE'S THE REAL DEAL, BUT YOU'RE ONLY AN IMITATION.

I'M NOT HER IMITATION. THE COMPANY MADE ME MIMIC JENNY YOU.
THE ONLY DIFFERENCE BETWEEN US IS THAT SHE CAME FIRST AND I CAME LATER.
GO AHEAD AND AUDITION.
IF YOU PASS THE AUDITION, I'LL TAKE YOU AS "ANGIE," NOT A COPY OF JENNY YOU.
YOU BET.

LOOK HOW SHE DRESSES. SHE'S A JENNY YOU WANNABE.
WOW, CUTE! SHE MUST BE NEW.
ANGIE, YOUR SINGLE IS ON ITS WAY TO NUMBER ONE. KEEP YOUR FINGERS CROSSED.
nine six newyork
nine six newyork
WHOA, WHAT A NICE WORLD. A WORLD WHERE A REPLICA BEATS THE ORIGINAL AND BECOMES NUMBER ONE.
JENNY'S EYES...
THOSE EYES WERE SAYING...
"HMPH! YOU'RE ONLY AN IMITATION!"
HOW ARE YOU?
YOU'VE NEVER MET ANGIE BEFORE?
nine six newyork
nine six newyork

I'M NOT A REPLICA OF JENNY YOU!!
I'LL SHOW HER. I'LL RISE AGAIN. I AM ANGIE.
I'M GOING TO BEAT JENNY YOU...!
NICE CLAUP

EUMPA. LET'S EAT.

I DON'T HAVE A LUNCH. NOBODY MAKES ME ONE...

THEN GET SOME INSTANT NOODLE SOUP FROM THE CAFETERIA. WE CAN STILL EAT TOGETHER.

Focused stare!

NO! MINE!

I'VE BEEN LIVING ON BREAD AND WATER. I WANT SOME RICE...

SOB! KIND CHANSUP...

HERE YOU GO.

IS IT GOOD?
Smack, Smack
DUDE, IT SURE IS. I LOVE POTATOES WITH SOY SAUCE!

BE AGGRESSIVE, DUDE! IF A GUY IS AGGRESSIVE, A GIRL'S BOUND TO GO OUT WITH HIM EVENTUALLY.
HOW?
Stick it out. ♡
THAT WAS MORE THAN I WANTED TO SEE.
YOU'RE A GUY. GUYS HAVE POWER. HAVEN'T YOU LEARNED ANYTHING FROM ME YET?
OUCH!
I NOTICED THAT A PRETTY BOY LIKE YOU HAS A HARDER TIME GETTING A GIRLFRIEND.
SO DO YOU, DUDE.
Chansup is always on the prowl for a girlfriend!
MAYBE IT'S YOUR LAID-BACK ATTITUDE THAT TURNS YOUNGJU OFF.
YOU'D BETTER LET HER KNOW HOW YOU FEEL.

HI, EUMPA! HAVE YOU EATEN LUNCH?
THERE SHE IS, DUDE. GO FOR IT!
YEP.
THIS DORK EUMPA ATE MY LUNCH.
HEE HEE!
ASK HER OUT! ASK HER OUT!
HEY, WHEN ARE YOU COMING TO MY STUDIO? YOU SAID YOU WANT TO SEE ME PRACTICE.
SOON. I'VE BEEN BUSY THESE DAYS.
WHY ARE YOU SO BUSY? MIDTERMS HAVE ALREADY PASSED.
WELL, JUST THIS AND THAT...HEE HEE HEE.

MUST BE SUPER BUSY TOO. I REALLY FEEL FOR YOU!
BUT I'M LOOKING FORWARD TO SEEING YOU ON TV.
I'VE ALREADY BRAGGED TO MY SIBLINGS...
...THAT MY FRIEND IS GOING TO BE A STAR.
DO YOU HAVE MANY SIBLINGS?
ONE YOUNGER BROTHER AND ONE YOUNGER SISTER. THEY'RE SO CUTE!
WHAT WAS THAT? I TOLD YOU TO ASK HER OUT SO YOU CAN SHOW HER YOUR MANLY SIDE.
BUT THEN YOU LET HER CONSOLE YOU INSTEAD.
THAT'S TYPICAL OF ME ANYWAY.

PHEW! I'M SO SLEEPY... EVERY DAY I PRACTICE UNTIL THE WEE HOURS, AND WAKE UP EARLY MORNING FOR JOGGING...
GAZING AT YOUNGJU MIGHT WAKE ME UP.
THIS MUST BE WHY JENNY AND HA ROCK SLEEP DURING THE CLASS...
YOUNGJU IS DOZING OFF, TOO. WE HAVE SOMETHING IN COMMON.
SO... CUTE...

HOW CAN I ASK HER...
Ding Dong
SCHOOL'S IN SESSION!
...TO GO OUT WITH ME?
JIHAE, I'M GOING OUT FOR A JOG.
DON'T WAKE ME UP!

I LOVE GOING FOR A RUN. IT REALLY FUELS ME.

COME TO THINK OF IT, IT'S BEEN AWHILE SINCE I WENT JOGGING...

I SHOULD BE DELIVERING NEWSPAPERS.

THEN I COULD MAKE SOME MONEY...

A GIRL DELIVERING NEWSPAPERS?!

THAT MUST BE DIFFICULT.

YOUNGJU?

CHANSUP, I NEED SOME ADVICE.

WHAT?! SHE WAS DELIVERING NEWSPAPERS?

PLEASE KEEP IT A SECRET.

WHAT DID YOUNGJU DO AFTERWARD?

SHE GOT FREAKED OUT AND RODE AWAY ON HER BICYCLE.

TODAY IN CLASS, SHE SEEMED SO EMBAR-RASSED.

SHE'S TOTALLY IGNORING ME. I DON'T KNOW WHAT TO SAY TO HER.

SHE MUST HAVE TROUBLES AT HOME.

THAT'S WHY SHE NEVER BRINGS HER LUNCH AND ALWAYS DOZES OFF DURING THE CLASS.

HOW DO YOU KNOW SO MUCH? DO YOU HAVE THE HOTS FOR HER OR SOMETHING?

HELLO! AM I YOU?
I LIKE TALL GIRLS WITH BIG BOOBS.
I'D NEVER GO FOR SUCH A TINY GIRL..
LOOK, I KNOW YOU LIKE HER. SINCE YOU'RE A BUSY GUY, I'VE BEEN KEEPING MY EYE ON HER FOR YOU.
CHANSUP ...
THANK YOU.
YOU'RE CREEPY, MAN. GO AWAY.
BUT LET'S FIGURE OUT HOW YOU CAN ASK HER OUT.
WE NEED TO THINK OF SOMETHING THAT WILL APPEAL TO HER SYMPATHY.
JUST ACT LIKE NOTHING HAPPENED.
GIVE HER THE IMPRESSION THAT YOU'LL ALWAYS BE ON HER SIDE NO MATTER WHAT.
GULP
YEAH, THAT'S IT!

CONFESS YOUR FEELINGS.
YOUNGJU... WELL...
UH, WILL YOU BUY ME SOME RICE?
I HAVEN'T HAD RICE IN A LONG TIME.
MY MOM IS TOO LAZY TO COOK IT FOR ME.
YOU SHOULDN'T TALK ABOUT YOUR MOM LIKE THAT.
YOU ONLY HAVE ONE MOM, YOU KNOW.
HEY, ARE YOU FINISHED WITH YOUR LUNCH? CAN I HAVE YOUR LEFTOVERS?
THAT'S GROSS!
NO, IT'S NOT GROSS AT ALL.

I GUESS IT'S TRUE THAT SKINNY PEOPLE EAT MORE.
MAYBE, BUT I'M STILL GROWING, DON'T YOU THINK? I MEAN, I'M ONLY 16.
WHAT, THAT YOUNG? I'M OLDER THAN YOU, THEN!
WELL, MISS OLDER WOMAN, THANKS FOR THE EATS!
HA HA...
ACTUALLY I WAS GOING TO TAKE YOU TO MY STUDIO AND LET YOU SEE MY DANCE ROUTINE.
BUT I'M STILL WAY TOO CLUMSY.
YOU'VE BEEN PRACTICING HARD, THOUGH.
I HAVE NO TALENT IN DANCING-- SO INSTEAD OF DANCING WELL, I'M TRYING TO DANCE CUTE.
HA HA! THAT SHOULDN'T BE TOO HARD.
WOULD YOU LIKE TO GO IN THERE? I'LL SHOW YOU WHAT I DO BEST.

태영 게임월드
24시간 영업

BEAT MANIA IS A HUGE HIT IN JAPAN NOW.

IF A GUY IS GOOD AT THIS, HE CAN GET ALL THE GIRLS!

LOOK. WHEN YOU SEE THE NOTE, YOU JUST HIT THE KEY ACCORDINGLY.

WHAT I'M PLAYING NOW IS ONLY LEVEL THREE. IT'S NOT VERY DIFFICULT, BUT IT'S THE SONG I LIKE.

beatstage 3rd MIX
LISTEN...
WHAT'S THE NAME OF THIS SONG?
IT'S GREAT. VERY BEAUTIFUL.

"DO YOU LOVE ME?"

DO YOU LOVE ME?

I DO.

YOU'RE THE ONE.

OHMIGOSH!

PLEASE PLAY "SKA A GO-GO."

CAN YOU PLAY "SKA"?

WOW! GREAT PLAY. CAN YOU PLAY SOMETHING ELSE?

PEOPLE STARTED GATHERING AROUND EUMPA LIKE CLOUDS, AND THEY GAVE HIM BIG CHEERS AND A STORM OF APPLAUSE (EVEN THOUGH IT WAS JUST A VIDEO GAME).
beatstage 3rd MIX
MAYBE THIS WAS EUMPA'S FIRST UNOFFICIAL DEBUT.
EUMPA CLEARED A DIFFICULT SONG IN LEVEL FIVE, SO I ASKED HIM OUT FOR A DATE.
WOW! GREAT!
CLEAR!
PLAY ANOTHER ONE. YOU'RE AWESOME.
AND FROM THAT DAY FORWARD, WE STARTED DATING...
SECTION 21 DO YOU LOVE ME?/ THE END

SECTION 22
FINAL FANTASY

MY MOM'S REALLY SICK.
HER STOMACH IS SO BLOATED, SHE LOOKS AS FAT AS A FROG.
BUT WE CAN'T AFFORD TO TAKE HER TO THE HOSPITAL OR PAY FOR HER MEDICINE.
SHE HAS TO TAKE WHAT THEY CALL ALBUMIN OR SOMETHING THAT COSTS THOUSANDS OF DOLLARS A DAY.

I DON'T CARE ABOUT HAVING TO WORK, BUT I'M SO AFRAID THAT I'LL LOSE MY MOM.
THAT THOUGHT SCARES ME SO MUCH THAT I WAKE UP IN A COLD SWEAT IN THE MIDDLE OF THE NIGHT.
I'LL ALWAYS BE ON YOUR SIDE.

I'LL BE RIGHT BESIDE YOU ALL THE TIME.
I'LL KEEP THIS PROMISE EVEN AFTER I GROW UP.

AS MY MOM HAS PROTECTED ME, I'LL PROTECT YOU.

HOWEVER, I WON'T LOVE YOU FROM AFAR AS MY MOM DOES.

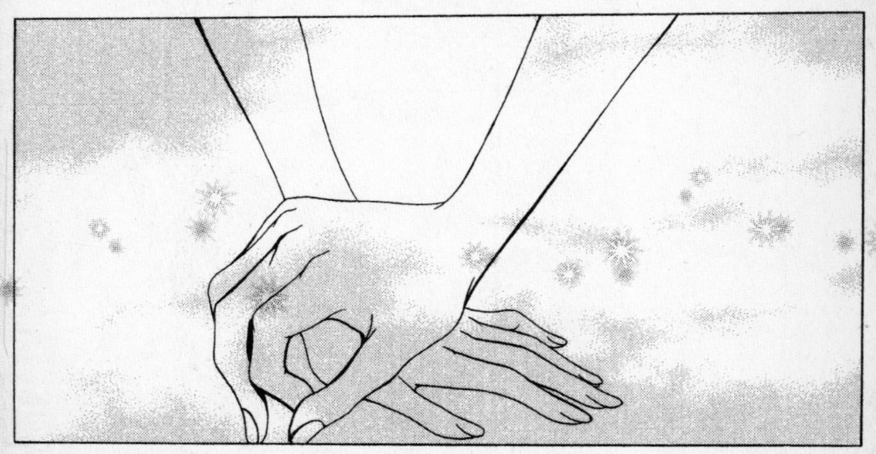

MR. YUNJIN LEE.
YUNJIN.
AH, MISS JAERONG.
REMEMBER THE IDEA YOU SUGGESTED TO ME THE OTHER DAY?
WE WANNA GO WITH IT.
THE PRESIDENT LIKED IT, AND THE TV STAFF FOUND IT FUNNY.
재롱
HOW ARE YOU? YOU SEEM BUSY.

AH, YOU GOT COSTUMES FOR TEAM TWO.
WAIT... I SHOULD CALL YOU D.E.Z. FROM NOW ON.
D.E.Z.?
IT'S SPELLED D.E.Z. AND PRONOUNCED AS "DAISY."
THAT'S THE OFFICIAL NAME FOR TEAM TWO.
THEY'RE MAKING THEIR DEBUT AS AN OPENING ACT AT JENNY'S SEOUL CONCERT.

AH, HERE YOU COME, YUNJIN AJEOCCI.
I TOLD YOU TO CALL ME HYOUNG.
SOOYONG, HAVE YOU DONE WHAT I TOLD YOU TO DO?
SURE, EXCEPT EUMPA...
I TOLD HIM TO KEEP PRACTICING DURING THE BREAK.

HE'S WAY BEHIND.
BUT HE CAME IN LATE TODAY.

HAVE PATIENCE. THAT'S WHAT A LEADER IS SUPPOSED TO DO.

PRESIDENT, I DON'T KNOW WHAT YOUR PLAN IS.
NEVER-THELESS, I'LL MAKE IT HAPPEN.
금연
SPORT
SPORT

AH, THERE YOU ARE. I'VE BEEN WAITING FOR YOU.
EUMPA?
SORRY. I CAN'T HELP YOU TODAY.
WHY NOT?

WE'RE MAKING OUR DEBUT...
...AS AN OPENING ACT FOR JENNY'S SEOUL CONCERT.
WE HAVE A NEW NAME, TOO. IT'S D.E.Z., DANGEROUS ETERNAL ZONE.
WE'VE SCHEDULED INTERVIEWS WITH MAGAZINES ALREADY.

I DIDN'T TELL YOU BECAUSE I WASN'T SURE UNTIL NOW.

SINCE TEAM ONE HAS ALREADY FINISHED THEIR CD, WE THOUGHT THEY'D DEBUT FIRST.

WE FIGURED OUR ODDS WERE QUITE LOW, ESPECIALLY SINCE WE HAVEN'T EVEN PRODUCED OUR CD YET.

BUT THE COMPANY DECIDED TO PUSH A GIRL GROUP FIRST.

I FEEL SO LUCKY. MY PARENTS WERE SO EXCITED!

CONGRATU-
LATIONS,
NUNA.
THANKS.
YOU SHOULD
COME, TOO.
OKAY?
EUMPA.
I'M LOOKING
FORWARD TO
SEEING YOU
ON TV.
SECTION 22 FINAL FANTASY/ THE END

Jenny You Concer
IN SEOUL
6 ~ 6.9

세종문화회관
WE LOVE JENNY
제니누나 사랑해

Jenny Y 
6.6 ~ 6.8
JENNY CONCERT
세종문화회관
Jenny You Official Fan Club
"Baby Doll"
We Love Jenny

HEY! WHAT'S UP? I'M INKYOUNG CHO...

...REPORTING TO YOU LIVE FROM SEOUL, THE LAST STOP ON JENNY'S NATIONAL TOUR. SBC WILL BRING YOU THIS HOT CONCERT FROM THE BEGINNING TO THE END!

HELLO, EVERYONE.
I LOVE YOU! JENNY'S COOL!!
GOSH! WHAT ARE YOU DOING HERE? ARE YOU ALSO A MEMBER OF THE JENNY YOU FAN CLUB?!
I LOVE YOU! JENNY'S COOL!!
Yikes—Mr. Nam, a famous TV host!
I CAME HERE TO SHOOT THE "SURPRISE STAR CAMERA"* PROGRAM FOR SBC.
GUESS WHAT?! WE AREN'T REALLY THE CONCERT CAMERA CREW—WE'RE THE "SURPRISE STAR CAMERA" CREW!
ARE YOU SURPRISED?
He even looks scary...
* Like the "Punk'D" of Korea!
NOW, WOULD YOU LIKE TO SEE THE BACKSTAGE? WE'RE HEADING TOWARD JENNY'S WAITING ROOM.
MR. NAM, FOLLOW ME WITH YOUR DISGUISE ON, PLEASE.

THIS IS JENNY'S WAITING ROOM.
MAKEUP? DISGUISE? JENNY'S IN THE MIDDLE OF SOMETHING. SHE SHOULDN'T SEE US YET, SO WE'LL STAY AWAY FROM HER AT THE MOMENT.
WHERE ARE WE NOW?
WHAT'S UP?!
RIGHT ON! THIS IS D.E.Z., THE BEAUTIFUL HIP-HOP BAND WHO'S OPENING FOR JENNY.

IT'S THE WAITING ROOM FOR JENNY'S BACKUP DANCERS.
YIKES, THESE GIRLS ARE HOT!
HMM... LET'S SEE WHERE WE ARE...
OH, MY GOD, IT'S WALL-TO-WALL HOTTIES IN HERE!!
OKAY, HERE'S A HINT: THE PLOT OF TONIGHT'S "SURPRISE STAR CAMERA" INVOLVES BACKUP DANCERS!
HERE'S A SCORCHING SWEETIE NOW. I'LL ASK HIM WHETHER HE'S CONFIDENT ABOUT OUR SNEAKY SCHEME.
HELLO?

AH?
HELLO?

SECTION 23
TURNING POINT

YOU LOOK SO PRETTY THAT I THOUGHT YOU WERE A GIRL.
I THINK YOU SHOULD BE A LEAD SINGER INSTEAD OF A BACKUP DANCER.
THAT'S MY GOAL.

LET'S TALK ABOUT WHAT'S GOING ON HERE.
DO YOU THINK THE PLAN WILL GO OFF WITHOUT A HITCH?
IT WILL.
WE'RE CONFIDENT!!

OKAY!
GREAT. I KNOW YOU'RE ALL DOING A GREAT JOB. JUST KEEP IT UP!
SURE.
LEAVE IT TO US.

HERE'S THE PLAN...
TOMORROW, JENNY'S STARTING HER THREE-DAY SEOUL CONCERT.
THE SBC CANDID CAMERA TEAM WILL BE THERE TO "PUNK" HER OUT!
JENNY WILL FREAK OUT!
IN THE BEGINNING, EVERYTHING WILL GO AS SCHEDULED. THEN IN THE MIDDLE OF THE CONCERT, A TOTALLY DIFFERENT TEAM OF BACKUP DANCERS WILL SHOW UP. THEY'LL START PERFORMING A DIFFERENT DANCE FROM THE PREVIOUSLY CHOREOGRAPHED ONE.
SHE WON'T KNOW WHAT THE HELL IS GOING ON!
THEN, THE BACKUP DANCERS WILL ALL START DOING THEIR OWN INDIVIDUAL DANCES, AND ONE OF THEM WILL GRAB THE MIKE AND START SINGING JENNY'S SONG HIMSELF.

JENNY WON'T KNOW WHAT HIT HER!
THESE BACKUP DANCERS WILL THEN TELL THE AUDIENCE THEY'RE MAKING THEIR CONCERT DEBUT.
...THAT WILL BE YOU GUYS.
...THE ONES WHO WILL STORM JENNY'S STAGE...
LOOK, THE GROUP OF BACKUP DANCERS...

TEAM TWO IS MAKING THEIR DEBUT BEFORE US.
AND A RIVAL PRODUCTION COMPANY IS FORMING ANOTHER BOY BAND.
WE MIGHT NOT HAVE ANOTHER CHANCE THIS YEAR.
BECAUSE OF MY ROAD MANAGER BACKGROUND, I DON'T HAVE MUCH PULL WITH THE RECORD COMPANY. THEY WON'T LISTEN TO MY SUGGESTIONS.
BUT I KNOW IN MY GUT THIS IS A GOLDEN OPPORTU-NITY.
NO MATTER WHAT, I'D LIKE YOU TO MAKE YOUR DEBUT NOW SO YOU'LL QUALIFY FOR THE BEST NEW POP ARTIST AWARD THIS YEAR.

GET NOTICED! AT ANY COST.
SHOW 'EM WHAT YOU'RE MADE OF AND CAPTURE THE HEARTS OF THE PUBLIC AND MEDIA.
HYOUNG, YOU DON'T HAVE TO DO THIS. YOU CAN JUST FOLLOW THE ORDERS OF THE PRODUCTION COMPANY AND GET PAID BY MANAGING OUR SCHEDULE.
WHY ARE YOU PLANNING SUCH AN EVENT, HYOUNG?
FIRST OF ALL, I'M YOUR MANAGER NOW.
SECOND OF ALL, I MAY NOT LOOK LIKE IT, BUT I'M AN AMBITIOUS MAN.

GET NOTICED!!
AT ANY COST,
GET SOME FREAKIN'
MEDIA ATTENTION!

안 내

HEY!

숙녀용 Woman

TISSUE

TISSUE

신사용 man

NUNA.

YOU CAME TO SEE ME. THANK YOU.
ACTUALLY I'M HERE BECAUSE I'M GOING ONSTAGE TOO.
WHAT? HOW COME I DIDN'T HEAR ABOUT IT...?
THIS STAGE JUST MIGHT BE THE PLACE YOU AND I BOTH MAKE OUR DEBUT.

YOU'VE HELPED ME SO MUCH.

NUNA, DON'T BE NERVOUS. CHEER UP AND DO YOUR BEST.
I'LL BE WATCHING YOU FROM BACKSTAGE.

AREN'T YOU NERVOUS?
I'M SO FREAKING NERVOUS!

NO. NOT AT ALL.
MAYBE IT'S BECAUSE THIS IS NOT MY OFFICIAL STAGE DEBUT.

JENNY YOU!!
JENNY COOL!!
JENNY YOU!!
PRINCESS
제니 짱
JENNY YOU!!
JENNY YOU!!

JENNY YOU!!
JENNY YOU!!
JENNY YOU!!

I'VE ALWAYS LIVED AS YOU TOLD ME.
HIP!!
HOP!!

I'M NO LONGER YOUR SWEET LITTLE GIRL.

YO!! WE ARE D.E.Z.! WE ARE DANGEROUS! WE ARE ETERNAL! WE ARE DANGEROUS! ETERNAL ZONE!

WHAT'S THIS? IT'S NOT JENNY YOU.

THE OPENING ACT!

THOSE GIRLS ARE DOING HIP-HOP?!

WHAT'S THAT? SCARY.

I DON'T LIKE THOSE GIRLS.

WHO WOULD LIKE GIRLS THAT SCARY?!

BABY DOLL

Jenny Cool

JENNY YOU !
JENNY YOU !
JENNY COOL!! JENNY YOU!!

JENNY COOL!!
JENNY COOL!!
JENNY
YOU!
JENNY YOU!!
JENNY YOU!!

JENNY YOU!! JENNY YOU!!

As all opening acts have experienced, D.E.Z. had to dance, sing and rap while being drowned out by an audience screaming the name of the main attraction.

JENNY COOL!! JENNY COOL!!

JENNY YOU!!

HELLO, EVERYONE. WE'RE MAKING OUR FIRST APPEARANCE TODAY. WE'RE A NEW GROUP, D.E.Z.

OUR TEAM NAME, D.E.Z., MEANS DANGEROUS ETERNAL ZONE...

JENNY YOU!! JENNY YOU!!

Nobody really paid any attention to the new band. This is a typical stage debut for any team.

MY NAME IS JEONGAH. I'M THE LEAD SINGER.

THIS IS SONYA, THE RAPPER.

JENNY YOU!!

JENNY WILL BE HERE SOON.

YO! ♡

How many people would even remember the name of this new band?

JENNY YOU!!

JENNY YOU!!

Their big debut that they've dreamed about their whole lives will end like this...

JENNY YOU!! JENNY YOU!!

JENNY YOU!! JENNY YOU!! JENNY YOU!!

The lights go off... The crowd goes wild!

The star makes her appearance like a queen.

SECTION 23 TURNING POINT/ THE END

유제니
JENNY YOU!
JENNY YOU!
JENNY!
I LOVE
YOU!!
유제니
유제니
I ♥ 제니
유제니
JENNY
YOU!
JENNY
YOU!

HERE'S A LITTLE SONG CALLED "COOL LOVE!"

SECTION 24
HEROINE

I'M WALKING ALONG THE STREET TONIGHT. I'M BAREFOOT.
SOMEBODY PUT A PAIR OF SHOES ON ME. PUT A PAIR OF GLASS SLIPPERS ON ME.

PLEASE TURN ME INTO YOUR CINDERELLA. I'M COLD. PLEASE MAKE ME HOT.
COOL LOVE. COOL LOVE. THIS IS COOL LOVE. YOUR TOUCH IS STILL COOL.
we LOVE 제니

COOL LOVE.
COOL LOVE.
YET IT IS
A WONDERFUL
LOVE...
WE LOVE JENNY

YOU'RE COLD YET ATTRACTIVE. SWIM TOWARD MY SEA OF 17. OH...COOL LOVE... IT'S SO COOL...
Jenny You Official Fan C
"Baby Doll"

I LOVE YOU.
YOU ARE SO COOL.
JENNY YOU!!
WELOVE유제니
바비인형
제니짱
LOVELY제니
JENNY, JENNY, JENNY!
WE LOVE YOU
WE LOVE JENNY!!

IS IT WHAT THEY CALL...
...BEING OVER-WHELMED?
SHE'S MAGNIFICENT!

THAT'S THE TALENT YOU HAVE, JENNY.
YOU SAID YOU DIDN'T HAVE THE CHARISMA TO BE A SUPERSTAR.
YOU ARE THE SUPER-STAR!!
JENNY!

NO MATTER HOW WONDERFUL THE CHOREO-GRAPHY IS...

...IT'S THE ARTIST WHO MAKES THE PERFORMANCE A MASTERPIECE OR TRASH. IT'S THE SIMPLE TRUTH.

JENNY PROVED IT TODAY.

NY

DON'T YOU WANT TO PUT A PAIR OF WINGS ON YOUR SHOULDERS AND FLY AWAY?
DON'T YOU WANT TO EXPRESS YOURSELF, YOUR MUSIC, EUMPA?

FLY
AWAY!!
LET'S FLY
TOGETHER!!

SEGONG CULTURAL CENTER
SEATING INFORMATION

YEAH!! AGAIN, THIS IS INKYOUNG CHO OF "STAR SURPRISE CAMERA."

GET READY TO GET PUNK'D, JENNY!

WOO-HOO! ♪

ALL NIGHT, JENNY YOU HAS SHOCKED AND TITILLATED THE AUDIENCE.

SHE CHANGED HER OUTFITS SO MANY TIMES, NO ONE CAN KEEP TRACK!

WHILE THE GUEST STAR IS PERFORMING, JENNY IS CHANGING COSTUMES AND RETOUCHING HER MAKEUP.

AH, SHE'S ALREADY FINISHED CHANGING HER DRESS, AND NOW SHE'S DOING HER MAKEUP.

SORRY TO ALL THE GUYS WHO HOPED TO GET A PEEP SHOW OUT THERE!

THE FIRST OPERATION IS UNDERWAY NOW...
HEY! MY 18'S LOVE. 18'S GOOD BYE.
LAUGHING WILDLY, SAYING GOODBYE.
JENNY'S MANAGER IS SINGING OUR PRANK SONG, "SWEET GOOD-BYE," USING WEIRD LYRICS.

AS TICKLISH AS POSSIBLE, GOODBYE... ♬ AS REVOLTING AS POSSIBLE, GOODBYE... ♬

HELLO?! I TOLD YOU TO STOP IT!

HER MANAGER DOESN'T LISTEN, AND KEEPS SINGING ANYWAY...

WHOA! THE GUEST STARS, T.N.T., HAVE FINISHED THEIR SONG ALREADY.

THANK YOU VERY MUCH. NOW IT'S TIME FOR JENNY YOU TO SAY GOODBYE... SWEET GOODBYE!

JENNY IS LED TO THE STAGE ESCORTED BY T.N.T.
GOODBYE MY 18'S LOVE. GOODBYE MY 18'S GOODBYE.
SHE'S COVERING HER EMBARRASSMENT BY STICKING OUT HER TONGUE SEXILY. A BEAUTIFUL GIRL CAN MAKE A MISTAKE AND STILL LOOK GOOD!
LAUGHING WILDLY, SAYING GOODBYE.
YES! THE INFLUENCE OF HER MANAGER'S REPEATED SINGING IS ALREADY SHOWING. JENNY JUST SANG THE WRONG LYRICS SHE'D HEARD BEFORE SHE CAME ONSTAGE!

TRYING TO SMILE AND SAY SOFTLY GOODBYE.

AS SWEET AS POSSIBLE GOODBYE.

YEAH. NOW, THE INTERLUDE... THE TEMPO BECOMES FASTER, AND OUR BACKUP DANCERS ARE GOING TO APPEAR.

YEAH!

EVEN IF THERE ARE TEARS IN MY EYES, SWEET GOODBYE.

유제니

NOW THAT SHE'S REGROUPED, JENNY IS SAYING GOODBYE TO T.N.T.

JENNY YOU.
JENNY YOU.
JENNY COOL.
JENNY COOL.
LOVE YOU!
GO!

SECTION 24 HEROINE/ THE END

SECTION
25 YOUR
MISTAKE

OKAY. THE INTERLUDE HAS STARTED...
NOW THE BACKUP DANCERS ARE COMING...

AND TEAM ONE... WHY...?
EUMPA...?

WHAT'S GOING ON?
THIS IS NOT THE RIGHT CHOREOGRAPHY! WHY ARE YOU DANCING DIFFERENTLY...?! WHY ARE EUMPA AND TEAM ONE HERE?!
HEE HEE HEE... SHE'S SO CUTE. SHE LOOKS PERFECTLY PETRIFIED. OUR PRETTY JENNY.
NEVERTHELESS, SHE'S TRYING HER BEST TO FOLLOW THE DANCE MOVES. I FEEL SORRY FOR HER.
NOW, THE FIRST BACKUP DANCER IS COMING TO THE FRONT TO STRUT HIS STUFF.

Windmill
HE'S HOT, TOO! WHO'S THAT?
WOW! WHO'S THAT? HE DANCES GREAT.
YOU'RE SO COOL!!

HE'S KNOWN TO BE THE BEST DANCER ON THE FARM TEAM. ISN'T HE INCREDIBLE?
FREEZE!
WAY INCREDIBLE!

HE'S FINALLY FINISHED, SO NOW IT'S THE RAPPER'S TURN.
HE'S ALSO A MEMBER OF ISSUE PRODUCTIONS' FARM TEAM. HE PASSED THE AUDITION IN THE UNITED STATES AND FLEW HERE. LISTEN TO HIS ENGLISH. ISN'T IT AMAZING? HE RAPS WITH PERFECTLY NATIVE PRONUNCIATION!
IN THE LIGHT OF DAY, HE HAS TO STUDY AWAY. HE'S GOT TO FIGHT THE SYSTEM THAT ALREADY DISSED HIM. HE WILL SURMISE WHAT'S TRUTH OR LIES.
Cool Song
WA HA HA... LOOK AT JENNY. SHE'S TOTALLY FROZEN BEHIND THEM.
HE HAS A VERY UNIQUE VOICE, DOESN'T HE?
.....

AFTER THE RAP... AS JENNY TRIES TO START HER SONG AGAIN...

TOTALLY IGNORING JENNY, EUMPA STARTS SINGING JENNY'S SONG...

FAREWELL... MY 18'S LOVE...

FAREWELL... MY 18'S GOODBYE... TRY TO SMILE AND SAY SOFTLY GOODBYE...

AS SWEET AS POSSIBLE GOODBYE...

THIS CHAP SEEMS SO AT EASE THAT HE EVEN THROWS A WINK AT JENNY. SO COOL!! I'LL BE HIS FAN.

EVEN IF THERE ARE TEARS IN MY EYES...

SWEET...

Good……

Bye…!!

YA-!!

KYAA!! WHO'S THAT KNOCKOUT?! SUCH A COOL VOICE!!
ISN'T IT A GIRL? SUPER-HIGH VOICE...
KYAA!!

WHO ARE YOU?
WOOO! WOOO! WOOOOOO!!
WHAAA!

PLEASE THINK ONE MORE TIME...
DO YOU REALLY WANT TO BREAK UP WITH ME...?
IF YOU WANT... AS YOU WISH. GOODBYE...
NEVERTHELESS...

I LOVE
YOU...

와아아아꺄아
와아
유제니 live!!
CONCERT!!

MISS JENNY, WE'RE SORRY. WE DIDN'T MEAN TO MAKE YOU CRY...
ARE YOU SURPRISED? YOU'RE ON "SURPRISE STAR CAMERA"!
JENNY, PLEASE STOP CRYING. IF YOU KEEP CRYING, WE'LL FEEL SO BAD!
I'M REALLY SORRY TO UPSET YOU SO MUCH.

I'M NOT CRYING 'CAUSE I'M UPSET.

IT'S THE SONG...

AH, YOU'RE CRYING BECAUSE YOU'RE SO IMPRESSED WITH THESE BOYS' PERFORMANCES! IT'S NOT WHAT WE EXPECTED... BUT, GUYS, YOU DID A GREAT JOB TODAY.
SEXY GIR
제니언니 I ♡You
ASK THEIR NAMES.
THEIR NAMES!
DON'T MAKE THEM GO. DO MORE.
THE AUDIENCE IS ASKING FOR THEIR NAME. DOES YOUR BAND HAVE A NAME YET?
THESE BOYS ARE MEMBERS OF A BOY BAND THAT ISSUE PRODUCTIONS IS PRODUCING.
NOT YET. OUR DEBUT IS NOT SCHEDULED, SO WE DON'T HAVE AN OFFICIAL BAND NAME YET... TEMPORARILY, WE'RE CALLED TEAM ONE.
FOR YOUR REFERENCE, I'M THE TEAM LEADER, SOOYONG KIM.
ONE! ONE!
ONE! ONE!
ONE RULES! ONE RULES!

AMAZING. THEY'RE GENERATING A HUGE RESPONSE EVEN BEFORE THEIR DEBUT.

YES...

ONE! ONE! ONE!

ONE!

ONE RULES! ONE RULES!

ONE! ONE!

YOU REALLY WORKED IT, YUNJIN.
AH... YES...

IT WENT EXACTLY AS YOU PLANNED!
CONSIDERING THE HUGE RESPONSE HERE, WE HAVE TO ACCELERATE OUR PLAN FOR ONE TO MAKE THEIR DEBUT AS SOON AS POSSIBLE.
IF NOT, THE MEDIA AND THE PUBLIC WON'T LEAVE US ALONE.

YOU TOOK MATTERS INTO YOUR OWN HANDS BECAUSE YOU THOUGHT I WASN'T RESPONSIVE.
AH...THAT'S NOT TRUE, PRESIDENT.

WHAT YOU DID TONIGHT WAS SEND A NAKED BABY TO THE WATER'S EDGE...
SOONER OR LATER, YOU'LL LEARN TO REGRET THIS.

SECTION 25 YOUR MISTAKE/ THE END

PRESIDENT, WAS TODAY'S EVENT INTENDED TO BE TEAM ONE'S SURPRISE DEBUT?
DOES ONE HAVE ONLY THREE MEMBERS? ARE THERE MORE?
WHEN WAS TEAM ONE FORMED AND TRAINED?
HAVE YOU SET THEIR OFFICIAL DEBUT SCHEDULE?
ARE YOU GOING TO SUPPORT ONE AS THE SUCCEEDING GROUP OF T.N.T.?
THERE'S A RUMOR THAT JAE YEE FROM T.N.T. HAS BEEN DRAFTED TO THE MILITARY. IS THIS T.N.T. BREAKUP RUMOR THE REASON FOR PUSHING ONE FORWARD?
BASED ON THE CHARACTERISTICS OF EACH BAND MEMBER, YOU OBVIOUSLY PLAN TO MAKE THEM A SUPER GROUP. ANY INFORMATION ABOUT THE MEMBERS...?!
JAE YEE'S MILITARY SERVICE HASN'T BEEN DECIDED.
THEREFORE, THE T.N.T. BREAKUP RUMOR IS NOT TRUE.
WE HAVEN'T SCHEDULED ONE'S DEBUT YET.

THEN WHAT'S THE REASON TO PROMOTE THE BAND SO HEAVILY THROUGH THE "SURPRISE STAR CAMERA" PRANK?
IT SEEMS LIKE YOUR DEBUT BAND, D.E.Z., COMPLETELY FAILED TO BE ACKNOWLEDGED.
I'LL MAKE A PUBLIC ANNOUNCEMENT LATER. THE ONLY INFORMATION I CAN PROVIDE TODAY IS ABOUT JENNY'S CONCERT TOUR AND D.E.Z.
WHAT YOU DID WAS TO SEND A NAKED BABY TO THE WATER'S EDGE...
SOONER OR LATER, YOU'LL LEARN TO REGRET THIS.

YOUR WORDS...
WHAT DID YOU MEAN BY THAT, PRESIDENT?

SECTION 26
YOU WERE
TRULY GREAT

WHOSE IDEA WAS IT?

THAT'S WHAT I THOUGHT.
MR. YUNJIN LEE'S... WHY?
Staff

JENNY. GIVE THEM SOME ENCOURAGING WORDS OR CONGRATULATIONS FOR THEIR DEBUT...

....

THEY LOOK PITIFULLY DOWN.

WHO ARE THESE GIRLS AGAIN?

IT WAS VERY... GREAT! WONDERFUL! IMPRESSIVE! FAB!

CONGRATS.

I DON'T REMEMBER THE NAME OF YOUR BAND, THOUGH.

JENNY!!

WHAT THE...?!

CALM DOWN!!

SOB!

DON'T CRY.

WHAT JENNY SAID IS RIGHT.

UM...

LET'S NOT FORGET TODAY'S HUMILIATION.

THAT WAY...
...WE WON'T HAVE A DAY LIKE THIS AGAIN.
JENNY, I TOLD YOU NOT TO MAKE ANY ENEMIES!
WHY ARE YOU SO MEAN TO YOUR OWN FAMILY?
WHY ASK? AS YOU SAID, I'M JUST BAD-TEMPERED.

DIDN'T YOU HEAR?
EUMPA'S THRILLING VOICE...
HIS ABILITY TO MAKE THE
SONG HIS OWN...
I RESPECT HIM,
AND I'VE BECOME MORE AND
MORE CRAZY ABOUT HIM.
BUT ALSO, THE JEALOUSY
DRIVES ME MAD.
I HAVE TO UNLEASH MY
WRATH ON SOMEBODY.

STOP LYING AND GO AWAY.

BELIEVE US, PLEASE.

STOP TRYING TO FOOL ME AND GO BACK TO YOUR SEATS AND WATCH THE SHOW. THESE LITTLE BRATS!
WHY ARE YOU BEATING ME? HMPH!

HMPH! WHAT THE HECK? IT'S NOT HIS CONCERT, BUT HE ALREADY INVITED HIS GIRLFRIEND BACKSTAGE?
HOW RUDE!
CUBS
GO AND TAKE THEM...
HEY!
YES?
...TO TEAM ONE'S DRESSING ROOM.

I'LL BE IN MY DRESSING ROOM.

WHAT?

Staff

GOOD WORK, JENNY. YOU'RE ALMOST DONE, SO CHEER UP!

NOW, IT'S TIME FOR THE FINALE.

BRING THE COSTUME. IT'LL TAKE AWHILE. HURRY!

OKAY, OKAY, HURRY, HURRY. PREPARE THE WIG-SETTING!

WELL DONE. EVEN THOUGH IT IRRITATED ME...
YOU WERE TRULY GREAT!

EUMPA!!
EUMPA, YOU WERE REALLY, REALLY WONDERFUL TODAY. I'M SO EXCITED! ♥
HEY, MR. COOL!!
DANIM
HOW DID YOU GET IN HERE?
WE CAME TO THE BACKSTAGE DOOR AND FOOLED THE GUARD.
WE TOLD HIM THAT YOU WERE SUPPOSED TO MEET US THERE. THAT YOU WOULD COME AND TAKE US IN...
OH MY GOD. HE PROBABLY HAS NO IDEA WHO I AM, RIGHT? HOW COULD YOU EVEN THINK YOUR PATHETIC LIE WOULD GET YOU IN?!
WELL, IT WORKED, DIDN'T IT?!

THE TRUTH IS...
...JENNY'S MANAGER BROUGHT US IN.
DON'T FOOL YOURSELF, YOUNGJU CHAE. I TOOK YOU TO EUMPA TODAY, BUT IT DOESN'T MEAN THAT I ACCEPT THE FACT THAT HE IS YOURS.
WELL, JENNY. IT'S YOUR FINALE. SMILE, BABE!
CHASE
LET'S HAVE A WONDERFUL WRAP PARTY!!
STEALING HIM FROM YOU WILL BE A LOT OF FUN, RIGHT?
WAY TO GO!

RIGHT! AFTER ALL, TOMORROW IS ANOTHER DAY.
TOMORROW, EUMPA WILL BE MINE!!

ENTERTAINMENT World

This week's title was written by Hodori.

AEIL SPORTS

nished Jenny's National Tour
, Sejong Cultural Center
V program's major events
needless to say, the world
rance of the band ONE
public attention
ed of the typical dance group formation
r, nevertheless, each individual plays
lity and talent is beyond
ny You and T.N.T. Profile.
sue Productions ambitiously presents
nuch anticipation on the future of ONE.

Journalist, Hodol Cheon

SUPER DANCE GROUP APPEARS

The New Band ONE's Surprise appearance at Jenny You's Concert.

Hello? Jadu!!

'Hello? Jadu!!' Vol. 3
ON SALE NOW!

Basic Skills for
Middle School Stude
Advanced Skills for
High School Studer

The First Translated Korean Version of the Most Acclaimed Japanese Bestseller W
The Giant, Sibata Renjaburo's lifetime masterpiece!

RUSH OF INQUIRIE
“WHO ARE THEY?”
ENTERTAINMENT
<T.N.T.> BREAKUP
Rising Star
SINCE THE BEGINNI
LEADER, JAE YEE'S M
SHOULD THEY BREA
SWARMED WITH PU
UNEXPECTEDLY, A
APPEARED AS A ST
NATURAL STAGE
SEEMS NOT TO B
ONLINE FAN CL
ASKING ABOUT
THE APPEARA
386세대의 우상, 안

HELLO. TODAY SPORTS.
MAY I SPEAK TO EUNMI PARK IN THE ENTERTAINMENT SECTION?
SHE'S NOT IN AT THE MOMENT.
투데이 신문사
투데이 신문사

IT'S ABOUT EUMPA WON, THE MEMBER OF ONE WHO WAS PROFILED IN TODAY'S PAPER.
UNFORTUNATELY, WE DON'T HAVE ANY INFORMATION ABOUT THE GROUP. AS SOON AS WE GET THE INFORMATION, WE'LL PUBLISH IT...
THAT'S NOT WHAT I'M CALLING FOR. I'D LIKE TO GIVE YOU SOME INSIDE INFORMATION ABOUT HIM.

HE'S WITH THE ACTRESS JIHAE HAN.

SECTION 26 YOU WERE TRULY GREAT/ THE END

SUPER SCANDAL!!

SUPER SCOOP?!

SECTION 27 I WOKE UP TO BE FAMOUS...?

A newly employed journalist received an anonymous phone call from Mr. X...

DID YOU TURN OFF THE GAS?
STOP GIVING ME SHIT!
YOU LEFT THE SHOWER ON LAST TIME.

WHAT ARE YOU GOING TO BUY? WHAT ARE YOU GOING TO MAKE FOR DINNER?
LET'S SEE WHAT LOOKS GOOD.
IF YOU MAKE A LIST BEFORE GROCERY SHOPPING, YOU'LL SAVE MONEY IN THE END.

WE CAN ALWAYS GO TO A RESTAURANT INSTEAD. I KNOW A PLACE WITH AWESOME STEAKS.

IT'S EXPENSIVE.

ARE YOU BUYING? NO! SO WHY DO YOU CARE?

HOO HOO HOO...

BECAUSE SOMEBODY JUST...

...TOOK A PICTURE OF US.

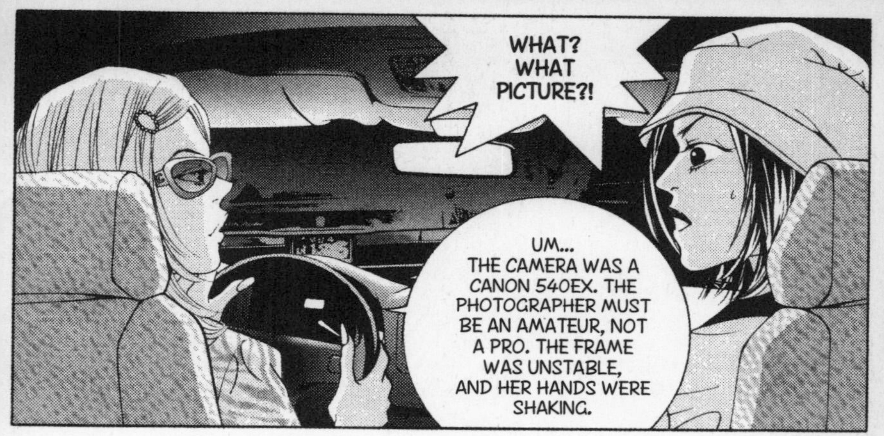

ARE YOU CRAZY? TURN AROUND. WE SHOULD GET THE FILM.

D-PULSE

IT'S FINE.

I TOLD HIM TO DO IT. I TOLD YUNJIN...

...TO USE ME.

WHY USE YOU, JIHAE?
WE LIVE TOGETHER.

YOU BECAME A BIG DEAL AFTER JENNY'S CONCERT. ON TOP OF THAT, THE FACT THAT YOU'RE LIVING WITH A CELEB LIKE ME CAN CAUSE A HUGE MEDIA FRENZY.

GOT IT? YOU CAN BECOME A STAR THIS WAY. THERE ARE MORE WAYS, TOO...
SOME OF THEM ARE EVEN DIRTIER...
WHAT WILL HAPPEN AFTER THE MEDIA FRENZY?
YOU'LL BE A STAR.

YOU SEE? I TOLD YOU BEFORE. THIS IS THE WORLD THAT YOU'VE PUT YOUR FEET IN.
THERE'S NO USE REGRETTING IT. JUST BECOME A STAR AT ANY COST!

THIS IS NOT...
WHAT?

THIS IS NOT...
THIS IS NOT WHAT I WANTED...

YUNJIN. WHERE'S YUNJIN?

HE'S WITH TEAM ONE AT THE BASEMENT STUDIO.

GET HIM ON THE PHONE. RIGHT NOW!

WHAT'S THE MATTER, PRESIDENT?
YOU'RE GOING TOO FAR.
He came really quickly.
DID YOU READ THIS?
Entertainment Like
MOVING WOMEN'S HEARTS WITH HIS EMOTIONAL ACT "LAST ROMANTIC"
......
12
Entertainment Like
waawaa
MOVING WOMEN'S HEARTS
WITH HIS EMOTIONAL ACT
"LAST ROMANTIC"

난, 오늘도 와와로 간다
waawaa
waawaa.com
http://www.waawaa.com
ENTERTAINMENT WORLD
Tinted Glasses
JIHAE HAN, SUGAR MAMA?
- LIVING WITH A MINOR -
EVEN THOUGH SHE'S WEARING A PAIR OF SUNGLASSES AND A CASUAL OUTFIT, IT'S EASY TO SEE THAT THIS WOMAN IS TOP ACTRESS JIHAE HAN. UNLIKE HER NAÏVE AND FRIENDLY IMAGE ON TV, SHE'S FAMOUS FOR HER LIBERAL LIFESTYLE AND STINGING TONGUE. THIS IS NOT A HOBBY BUT A CRIME. THE BOY WHO'S LIVING WITH JIHAE HAN IS A MEMBER OF A NEW GROUP, ONE. HE'S ALSO A ROOKIE STAR WHO ATTRACTED PUBLIC ATTENTION AND RECORDING INDUSTRY INTEREST AT JENNY YOU'S CONCERT. THERE ARE MANY RUMORS CONCERNING THEIR LIVING ARRANGEMENTS. ONE OF THEM IS THAT JIHAE HAN IS LIVING WITH THE BOY AND IS HIS GUARDIAN. THE OTHER IS THAT THEY'RE IN LOVE. MAYBE THIS MAY/DECEMBE ROMANCE IS OKAY...BUT PEOPLE ARE HOTLY ACCUSING JIHAE HAN FOR BEING A MAJOR CRADLE-ROBBER!
JOURNALIST, HOSOOK CHEON.
원작자 집서 드라마 촬영
S-TV 새일요극 '달콤한 신부' 야외세트장 사용
문희준 "빨리 팬들앞에
부상 예상외로 호전 '퇴원'
내달 중순께 활동재개할 듯
눈의 힘

THIS... THIS IS...

GREAT. HE'S FEATURED ON THE FRONT PAGE OF THE ENTERTAINMENT SECTION!

AND WE HAVEN'T EVEN SPENT A DIME ON PR. IT'S A GREAT STRATEGY.

Entertainment Like

MOVING WOMEN'S HEARTS WITH HIS EMOTIONAL ACT "LAST ROMANTIC"

DIDN'T I TELL YOU? ONE IS NOT GOING TO DEBUT ANYTIME SOON.

ARE YOU REBELLING AGAINST ME? WHAT ARE YOU GOING TO DO ABOUT THIS?! THIS ISN'T JUST AN ISSUE... IT'S A SCANDAL!

TO A YOUNG SINGER, A SCANDAL ABOUT A WOMAN IS CAREER POISON.

GREAT. BEFORE MAKING HIS DEBUT AS A SINGER, HE'S DEBUTING WITH SCANDAL.

IT'S NOT ME.
THEN WHO IS IT? WHEN WE SIGNED OUR CONTRACT, THERE WAS ONLY YOU AND ME AND ILIM. ARE YOU SAYING THAT ILIM DID THIS?!

PRESIDENT. I DIDN'T DO IT.
I KNOW. WHO SAID YOU DID? I WAS BEING SARCASTIC.

WHO'S THE JOURNALIST? CALL HER UP.
YES.
I MEAN IT, IT'S NOT ME. EVEN THOUGH JIHAE TOLD ME TO USE HER, I DIDN'T.
WHY WOULD I...

...DO ANYTHING THAT COULD HARM JIHAE?!

HEY. DID YOU READ THE NEWSPAPER?
EUMPA WON IS LIVING WITH JIHAE HAN.
m·net
HAVEN'T YOU HEARD THAT JIHAE HAN IS KNOWN AS THE "PRETTY BOY KILLER"? SHE'S NOTORIOUS.
← HERE, WE SEE "SMOKE WITHOUT FIRE."
SHUT UP. YOU ARE SMART ENOUGH TO KNOW THAT THE TABLOIDS ARE NOT TRUSTWORTHY.
Entertainment Like
MOVING WOMEN'S HEARTS WITH HIS EMOTIONAL ACT
BUT IT WAS MENTIONED ON ENTERTAINMENT LIVE TOO!
EVERY-BODY'S MAKING A FUSS ABOUT THIS SCANDAL.
HEY, JENNY YOU. DID YOU SEE THE PAPER?

CONSIDERING YOU STILL BELIEVE THOSE PAPERS, YOU MIGHT BE MORE NAÏVE THAN I THOUGHT.
NO, I ONLY BELIEVE WHAT I SEE.
I SAW THEM.
WHAT? DID YOU SEE THEM?
Ha Rock is suddenly the man in the know!
WHERE DID YOU SEE THEM?
WHERE? IS IT REALLY TRUE?

I WASN'T SURE AT FIRST.
BUT I CONFIRMED THE FACT RECENTLY.
IT'LL BE DIFFICULT TO WORK AS A MEMBER OF A NEW PRETTY-BOY DANCE GROUP AFTER THIS KIND OF DIRTY SCANDAL.
THAT'LL BE CRUCIAL.
HE MIGHT GET KICKED OUT OF SCHOOL, RIGHT?
...LIKE SCREWING YOUR MOM!
WELL, KIDS THESE DAYS ARE SO DARING. BUT SLEEPING WITH AN OLDER WOMAN IS...

I CAN'T BELIEVE IT...
NEVER...
I LEFT HIM ALONE WITH YOUNGJU BECAUSE IT'S YOUNGJU.
WHY OF ALL PEOPLE DOES HE HAVE TO BE WITH JIHAE, A WOMAN I TOTALLY HATE?
SHE'S SHAKING ...
BUT WITH THIS MIDDLE-AGED SLUT?
SHE HAS A TERRIBLE PERSONALITY, A DIVA COMPLEX AND A SHITTY ATTITUDE!
Meow! A middle-aged slut...

HOW FAR DID THEY GO?

LIVING TOGETHER?

WHY DO YOU HATE EUMPA SO MUCH?
I HATE ALL GUYS!
YOU'RE IN DENIAL. IN FACT, YOU'RE INTERESTED IN HIM, AREN'T YOU?
HUH?♡
I KNOW THAT YOU HAVE A CRUSH ON EUMPA.
WHAT ARE YOU SAYING?!
THE MOST BEAUTIFUL THING IN THE WORLD IS UNATTAINABLE LOVE. IT'S MORE BEAUTIFUL BECAUSE IT'S IMPOSSIBLE TO OBTAIN.

GOOD LUCK, MR. IN-THE-CLOSET!
SH-SHUT UP!! HOW DARE YOU CALL ME GAY!

I WON'T LEAVE YOU ALONE, EUMPA WON. CALLING A NEWSPAPER WAS JUST AN APPETIZER. THE MAIN DISH WILL BE WAITING FOR YOU. JUST WAIT AND SEE!!
HA ROCK MUST BE THE ONE WHO CALLED THE NEWSPAPER.
WASN'T IT OBVIOUS?
PRESIDENT. MISS JIHAE HAN IS HAVING A TV INTERVIEW WITH ENTERTAINMENT LIVE TO EXPLAIN HER SIDE OF THE SCANDAL TODAY.
WHAT IS THERE TO EXPLAIN?
I DON'T KNOW. JIHAE HAN'S AGENCY IS RATHER CALM, THOUGH...
...DESPITE THE FACT THAT ALL THE SALES OF THE PRODUCTS THAT JIHAE HAN ENDORSES HAVE DROPPED NOTICEABLY AFTER THE SCANDAL...

IT'S OBVIOUS THAT JIHAE HAN GOT MORE DAMAGE FROM THE SCANDAL THAN EUMPA.

SHE IS NOTORIOUS FOR HER LIBERAL LIFESTYLE AND SHARP TONGUE. HOWEVER, THIS IS A SCANDAL THAT INVOLVES A MINOR.

WHAT DID EUMPA SAY, YUNJIN?
HE SAID THEIR RELATIONSHIP IS NOTHING LIKE WHAT PEOPLE SAY.
YOU NEVER CAN TELL ABOUT PEOPLE, CAN YOU?
HOW COULD A BOY SO YOUNG AND DECENT DO SUCH A THING?

SINCE JIHAE HAN IS SO CRAFTY, SHE MIGHT BE ABLE TO SPIN THIS IN HER FAVOR.
BUT STILL, IT'S A HUGE BLOW TO US.
HOW CAN WE DEAL WITH THIS?

HELLO. THIS IS ENTERTAINMENT LIVE "CASE REPORT." AT THE MOMENT, THE BIGGEST SCANDAL IN THE INDUSTRY IS THE RUMOR THAT TOP TV STAR JIHAE HAN IS LIVING IN SIN WITH A MINOR.
IN ORDER TO CLEAR HER NAME, JIHAE HAN TALKS WITH US TONIGHT IN THE STUDIO... LIVE!
HOW ARE YOU? THANK YOU FOR COMING TO OUR SHOW.
NOT AT ALL.
FIRST OF ALL, LET'S CONFIRM WHETHER THE RUMOR IS TRUE OR FALSE.
IS IT TRUE?
IN A WAY, YES. WE LIVE TOGETHER.
ARE YOU SAYING THAT YOU LIVE WITH A BOY, BUT YOUR RELATIONSHIP WITH HIM IS NOT WHAT PEOPLE SAY?
HMM...?
WELL, I DON'T KNOW EXACTLY WHAT PEOPLE SAY, BUT IF WHAT THEY SAY IS TRUE, I'D BE A CRIMINAL.

WELL...
AFTER ALL, THE BOY I'M LIVING WITH IS A MINOR.
WELL, THE FACT IS...
TELL US WHAT'S REALLY GOING ON!
ARE YOU SAYING THAT YOU'RE NOT HIS LOVER BUT JUST A FRIEND OR GUARDIAN?
...HE IS MY NEPHEW.

SECTION 27
I WOKE UP TO BE FAMOUS...?/THE END

ONE VOLUME 4 – THE END

The Hits Keep Coming in the Next Volume of...

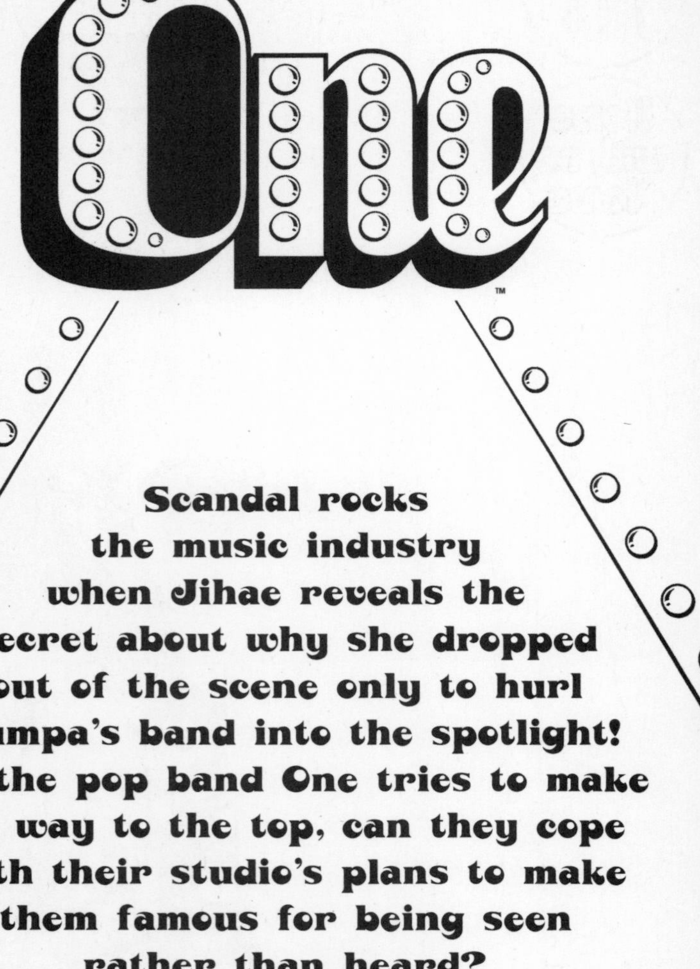

Scandal rocks the music industry when Jihae reveals the secret about why she dropped out of the scene only to hurl Eumpa's band into the spotlight! As the pop band One tries to make its way to the top, can they cope with their studio's plans to make them famous for being seen rather than heard?

A MUST HAVE PREQUEL TO THE BEST-SELLING SERIES

Horse with no Name

Every great love story has a beginning.

This special edition also includes two original tales!

© Fuyumi Soryo. ©2004 TOKYOPOP Inc. All Rights Reserved.

www.TOKYOPOP.com

TOKYOPOP®

© Maki Murakami • TOKYOPOP is a registered trademark of Mixx Entertainment, Inc. All Rights Reserved.

www.TOKYOPOP.com

By Koge-Donbo - Creator of Digicharat

The girl next door is
bringing a touch of heaven
to the neighborhood.

www.TOKYOPOP.com

©2003 Koge-Donbo. ©2004 TOKYOPOP Inc. All Rights Reserved.

TOKYOPOP®

TOKYOPOP®

Princess Ai™

A Diva torn from Chaos...
A Savior doomed to Love

Created by
Courtney Love
and D.J. Milky

©2003 TOKYOPOP Inc. and Kitty Radio, Inc. All Rights Reserved.

www.TOKYOPOP.com

An ordinary student
with an extraordinary gift...
TOKYOPOP
Eerie Queerie!™
He's there for you in spirit.
OT
OLDER TEEN
AGE 16+
www.TOKYOPOP.com
©2001 Shuri Shiozu. ©2004 TOKYOPOP Inc. All rights reserved.

TOKYOPOP®

Fruits Basket™

Life in the Sohma household can be a real zoo!

www.TOKYOPOP.com

©2003 Natsuki Takaya

kare kano

his and her circumstances

Story by Masami Tsuda

Life Was A Popularity Contest For Yukino.
Somebody Is About To Steal Her Crown.

Available Now At Your Favorite Book And Comic Stores!

KARESHI KANOJO NO JIJYO by Masami Tsuda
© 1994 Masami Tsuda. Copyright © 2003 TOKYOPOP Inc.
All rights reserved

www.TOKYOPOP.com

TOKYOPOP®

ALSO AVAILABLE FROM TOKYOPOP®

MANGA

.HACK//LEGEND OF THE TWILIGHT
@LARGE
ABENOBASHI: MAGICAL SHOPPING ARCADE
A.I. LOVE YOU
AI YORI AOSHI
ANGELIC LAYER
ARM OF KANNON
BABY BIRTH
BATTLE ROYALE
BATTLE VIXENS
BOYS BE...
BRAIN POWERED
BRIGADOON
B'TX
CANDIDATE FOR GODDESS, THE
CARDCAPTOR SAKURA
CARDCAPTOR SAKURA - MASTER OF THE CLOW
CHOBITS
CHRONICLES OF THE CURSED SWORD
CLAMP SCHOOL DETECTIVES
CLOVER
COMIC PARTY
CONFIDENTIAL CONFESSIONS
CORRECTOR YUI
COWBOY BEBOP
COWBOY BEBOP: SHOOTING STAR
CRAZY LOVE STORY
CRESCENT MOON
CROSS
CULDCEPT
CYBORG 009
D•N•ANGEL
DEMON DIARY
DEMON ORORON, THE
DEUS VITAE
DIABOLO
DIGIMON
DIGIMON TAMERS
DIGIMON ZERO TWO
DOLL
DRAGON HUNTER
DRAGON KNIGHTS
DRAGON VOICE
DREAM SAGA
DUKLYON: CLAMP SCHOOL DEFENDERS
EERIE QUEERIE!
ERICA SAKURAZAWA: COLLECTED WORKS
ET CETERA
ETERNITY
EVIL'S RETURN
FAERIES' LANDING
FAKE
FLCL
FLOWER OF THE DEEP SLEEP, THE
FORBIDDEN DANCE
FRUITS BASKET
G GUNDAM
GATEKEEPERS
GETBACKERS
GIRL GOT GAME
GRAVITATION
GTO
GUNDAM SEED ASTRAY
GUNDAM WING
GUNDAM WING: BATTLEFIELD OF PACIFISTS
GUNDAM WING: ENDLESS WALTZ
GUNDAM WING: THE LAST OUTPOST (G-UNIT)
HANDS OFF!
HAPPY MANIA
HARLEM BEAT
HYPER RUNE
I.N.V.U.
IMMORTAL RAIN
INITIAL D
INSTANT TEEN: JUST ADD NUTS
ISLAND
JING: KING OF BANDITS
JING: KING OF BANDITS - TWILIGHT TALES
JULINE
KARE KANO
KILL ME, KISS ME
KINDAICHI CASE FILES, THE
KING OF HELL
KODOCHA: SANA'S STAGE
LAMENT OF THE LAMB
LEGAL DRUG
LEGEND OF CHUN HYANG, THE
LES BIJOUX
LOVE HINA
LOVE OR MONEY
LUPIN III
LUPIN III: WORLD'S MOST WANTED
MAGIC KNIGHT RAYEARTH I
MAGIC KNIGHT RAYEARTH II
MAHOROMATIC: AUTOMATIC MAIDEN
MAN OF MANY FACES
MARMALADE BOY
MARS
MARS: HORSE WITH NO NAME
MINK
MIRACLE GIRLS
MIYUKI-CHAN IN WONDERLAND
MODEL
MOURYOU KIDEN: LEGEND OF THE NYMPHS
NECK AND NECK
ONE
ONE I LOVE, THE
PARADISE KISS
PARASYTE
PASSION FRUIT
PEACH GIRL
PEACH GIRL: CHANGE OF HEART
PET SHOP OF HORRORS
PITA-TEN

07.15.04T

ALSO AVAILABLE FROM TOKYOPOP®

PLANET LADDER
PLANETES
PRESIDENT DAD
PRIEST
PRINCESS AI
PSYCHIC ACADEMY
QUEEN'S KNIGHT, THE
RAGNAROK
RAVE MASTER
REALITY CHECK
REBIRTH
REBOUND
REMOTE
RISING STARS OF MANGA
SABER MARIONETTE J
SAILOR MOON
SAINT TAIL
SAIYUKI
SAMURAI DEEPER KYO
SAMURAI GIRL REAL BOUT HIGH SCHOOL
SCRYED
SEIKAI TRILOGY, THE
SGT. FROG
SHAOLIN SISTERS
SHIRAHIME-SYO: SNOW GODDESS TALES
SHUTTERBOX
SKULL MAN, THE
SNOW DROP
SORCERER HUNTERS
STONE
SUIKODEN III
SUKI
THREADS OF TIME
TOKYO BABYLON
TOKYO MEW MEW
TOKYO TRIBES
TRAMPS LIKE US
UNDER THE GLASS MOON
VAMPIRE GAME
VISION OF ESCAFLOWNE, THE
WARRIORS OF TAO
WILD ACT
WISH
WORLD OF HARTZ
X-DAY
ZODIAC P.I.

NOVELS

CLAMP SCHOOL PARANORMAL INVESTIGATORS
SAILOR MOON
SLAYERS

ART BOOKS

ART OF CARDCAPTOR SAKURA
ART OF MAGIC KNIGHT RAYEARTH, THE
PEACH: MIWA UEDA ILLUSTRATIONS

ANIME GUIDES

COWBOY BEBOP
GUNDAM TECHNICAL MANUALS
SAILOR MOON SCOUT GUIDES

TOKYOPOP KIDS

STRAY SHEEP

CINE-MANGA™

ALADDIN
CARDCAPTORS
DUEL MASTERS
FAIRLY ODDPARENTS, THE
FAMILY GUY
FINDING NEMO
G.I. JOE SPY TROOPS
GREATEST STARS OF THE NBA: SHAQUILLE O'NEAL
GREATEST STARS OF THE NBA: TIM DUNCAN
JACKIE CHAN ADVENTURES
JIMMY NEUTRON: BOY GENIUS, THE ADVENTURES OF
KIM POSSIBLE
LILO & STITCH: THE SERIES
LIZZIE MCGUIRE
LIZZIE MCGUIRE MOVIE, THE
MALCOLM IN THE MIDDLE
POWER RANGERS: DINO THUNDER
POWER RANGERS: NINJA STORM
PRINCESS DIARIES 2
RAVE MASTER
SHREK 2
SIMPLE LIFE, THE
SPONGEBOB SQUAREPANTS
SPY KIDS 2
SPY KIDS 3-D: GAME OVER
TEENAGE MUTANT NINJA TURTLES
THAT'S SO RAVEN
TOTALLY SPIES
TRANSFORMERS: ARMADA
TRANSFORMERS: ENERGON

You want it? We got it!
A full range of TOKYOPOP products are available now at:
www.TOKYOPOP.com/shop

07.15.04T

TOKYOPOP®

CONFIDENTIAL CONFESSIONS

By REIKO MOMOCHI

REAL TEENS.
REAL PROBLEMS.
REAL MANGA.

品質第一公式商品
100%
AUTHENTIC
MANGA

AVAILABLE NOW
AT YOUR FAVORITE
BOOK AND COMIC STORES

©REIKO MOMOCHI
TOKYOPOP is a registered trademark of Mixx Entertainment, Inc.

www.TOKYOPOP.com